AWOL

By Rob Gee

First Published in the UK in 2024 by Mantle Lane Press

ISBN 978-1-9160570-9-8

Mantle Lane Press
Mantle Arts
Springboard Centre
Mantle Lane
Coalville
LE67 3DW
www.mantlelanepress.co.uk

Printed and bound in Canada by Hignell Book Printing

Cover design and interior layout Matthew Pegg
www.mpegg.co.uk

Image Credits
Front Cover: Road sign graphic: Woody Kitson: ekit.co.uk
Road sign: Clker-Free-Vector-Images. Pixabay
Sky photo: Mint Foto. Pixabay.
Back Cover: Performer photo: Ross den Otter: pinkmonkeystudios.com
Badge Flames: Stephen Steffler. Pixabay

For my parents, Glenda and Peter.

Any resemblance to the two main characters is purely a coincidence and that's a promise.

Contents

Rob Gee was a mental health nurse, then a comedian, and now a stand-up poet who dabbles in theatre. He's performed at over a hundred fringe festivals worldwide and regularly leads comedy and poetry workshops in mental health settings. Awards for solo shows include Best of Fest at Winnipeg, Saskatoon and Calgary Fringe Festivals, Best Solo Comedy at Buxton Fringe and Fringe Favourite at Limerick Fringe. Poetry slam victories include the Edinburgh Slam, BBC Two's Why Poetry Matters Slam, the Toronto $83 Slam and the Orlando Poetry Smackdown. He is also sent into schools as a warning to children.

Also by Rob Gee:

Forget Me Not: The Alzheimer's Whodunnit
Kevin, King of Egypt
My Daughter is a Donington Goth
Pig on the Wall
The Day My Head Exploded

Further details:
robgee.co.uk or
mantlelanepress.co.uk

Characters

In order of appearance

Cyril	A curmudgeonly gentleman with a critical mind.
Neville	A man who's learned to enjoy life's pleasures.
Hastings	His wife is always waiting for him.
Belinda	She's in charge and she isn't happy.
Patrick	The stoner care assistant.
Lily	An aspiring rock star with a confidence crisis.
Trevor	The leader of a biker gang.
Volunteer	Trained in first aid for all the wrong reasons.
Menu Man	An example to us all. Not necessarily a good one.
Biker Bloke	His only purpose is to hold Cyril's leg.
Rock Star	Even he doesn't know who he is.

Loosely based on a nearly true story.

Prologue

“Wisdom doesn’t necessarily come with age.
Sometimes age just shows up all by itself.”
Tom Wilson

Cyril and Neville appear.

Cyril
When I was young,
I could outrun
just about anything with legs
and several things with wheels.
Now here I am, aged eighty-two,
being chased through
an overcrowded field
full of people in leather.

Even the bald ones need a haircut,
and quite a few would benefit
from a good scrub down with a wire brush.

When did denim become so popular?
None of them are cowboys.
Neville’s right beside me.
We’re heading towards the horrendous noise.

I’ve never seen Neville run before.
It’s like a seagull failing to take off.

We reach the base of the viewing platform.

Neville shows the security man his pass.
I fumble and find mine. He lets us both past.

We head up the ramp. I turn around
and see the fluorescent vests
coming towards us through the crowd.

As soon as they come up here, we'll have nowhere to go.
I look at Neville and both of us know
what the other is thinking.
We make a decision and cross over to the scaffolding.

And, as they pass the security man and head up the ramp,
we start climbing up towards the speaker stack.
Neville gives me a smile and says there's no going back.

I take a moment to look around.
I've never seen so many people
pulsating as one to the most terrible sound.
Some of them see us and start to clap.
If these are my final moments on earth,
it's a crying shame the music's so crap.

Neville
I don't think I've ever seen such a wonderful view.
There's so much joy in humanity.
And beyond this tribe is rolling countryside
and fields as far as the eye can see.

It's such a blue sky.
I'll settle for that if this is it.
Down there is the mosh pit:
a human tsunami of balmy testosterone.
Maybe you're safer in the middle than you are around the edge.

I look at Cyril. He scratches his head
and smiles. *(Cyril doesn't smile.)*
He's a tricky fellow at times, but he is worthwhile.

We look down at the crowd and then at each other.

Cyril
And as our pursuers come towards us,
we throw ourselves into the air
and fly down towards all that filthy denim.

Neville
I can't see Cyril, but I'm glad I'm with him.

Two weeks earlier…

Act One

The Home

"You're not old until regrets take the place of dreams."
John Barrymore

Scene One

Hastings
I hope the bus arrives soon, or I'll be late for dinner. Margaret will be worried about me. She does witter on sometimes.

I do love her dearly, though. I was never much use as a single man. I was a terrible dancer. Terrible! I could clear a dancefloor in seconds. That's how I knew Margaret was the one for me: because she didn't care. She'd stay with me on that dancefloor, no matter how many times I farted.

Well, here's me getting all emotional. We've been waiting here a while now, haven't we?

Enter Patrick.

Hastings
Am I going home, or am I on my way to work?

Patrick
Mr Hastings? It's me, Patrick. I thought we'd find you here. Come on then. Margaret's this way.

Hastings
Are you sure? I'm getting the bus.

Patrick
You've arrived, Mr Hastings. Everything's okay.

Patrick walks Hastings away from the bus stop.

Scene Two

Cyril
Ah, they've got him, look. Poor old Hastings. I tell you what, Neville, that fake bus stop is saving them quite a bit of money. I bet the police are pleased they don't have to scramble a chopper every time someone buggers off.

Neville
Why do they always go to the bus stop?

Cyril
Well, I won't. When the time comes for me to do my runner, I'll have it wedged firmly in my head that that bus stop is less genuine than a smile on a bank manager. I'll give it a wide berth, let me tell you.

Neville
That's what Hastings used to say. He forgot and so will you. They'll collect you from that bus stop just the same as the rest of them. I don't think you'd be very good company at a bus stop.

Cyril
I'll write myself a note. I'll write a note and keep it in my wallet.

Neville
Yes. And then you'll be demanding to know why someone's written a note in your handwriting, and that'll make you very cross, and you'll be even worse company at the bus stop.

Anyway, you do that if you like. I'll stay where I am, in a soft waterproof chair, receiving care that's of a vaguely acceptable standard. I think it's important to enjoy what you've got in life.

Cyril
Neville is content to the point of being completely fuckwitted.
He always has to see the best in everyone.
It took us quite a while to learn how to get on,

but when you're in here, sooner or later,
you don't have a choice.
There's me and Neville
and a few other old boys
who still have… *(Looks at Neville.)* most of our marbles,
and everyone else is a woman.

And that's nice,
but there are some things you just don't talk about,
like the workings of your bladder,
which become a remarkable source of interest as you get older.

Neville and I are quite familiar with each other's waterworks
and that isn't something of which we're proud.
Well, I'm not.
Yes, Neville is content with the bladder he's got.

Scene Three

'Invisible Touch' by Genesis is playing.

Belinda
Hello, and welcome to Primrose House, where our residents have a relatively high level of functioning, thanks to us. My name's Belinda and I'm in charge.

Neville
She's not, you know.

Belinda
This is Cyril and Neville, two of our more established residents. Hello, gentlemen.

Neville waves, Cyril presents a finger.

Belinda
These people are from the Care Quality Commission. Just checking up on us.

Neville raises his hand.

Belinda
No, they won't want to talk to you.
Oh, you will? Oh good. We'll definitely make time for that.

But first, my colleague, Gavin, has organised three different playlists, so they don't get bored. Phil Collins and Genesis are on all of them. I mean they were quite big when they were in their forties.

As you can see,
we hook the sound up to the karaoke,
and, if you look, you can see the ball following the words…

Cyril glares at Neville who is lip-syncing.

Belinda
It's like poetry.
And over this way is Venetia House.
That's our higher dependency facility. *(Exits.)*

Cyril
Venetia House:
an ever-shrinking hell den of half-remembered realities.
Life clings to the residents there like a disease.

Neville
Belinda particularly enjoys it there, because no one can answer her back.

Cyril
We don't know much about Belinda, but she doesn't have a wedding ring and she was recently dropped off here by a woman.

Neville
We think she might be part of the BLT community.

Cyril
At least that would give us something to like about her.

Neville
You won't let them take me to Venetia House, will you, Cyril?

Cyril
Of course not, Neville. It wouldn't be fair on them.

Neville
Hmm. Is Lily visiting you this afternoon?

Cyril
I don't know. What day is it?

Neville
I couldn't tell you.

Cyril
Well, what's for dinner?

Neville
Hold on… shepherd's pie.

Both
Wednesday.

Neville
If she does come, do you still want me to pretend to, you know?

Cyril
Oh, yes please. I'll give you my apple strudel, unless of course there's anything else you'd fancy from the dismal repertoire of vaguely edible shittery that passes for food around here.

Neville
I don't like doing it, Cyril. It feels wrong.

Cyril
She's *my* granddaughter, I think it's for me to decide whether it's wrong or not.

It's fine.

Scene Four

Neville is looking vacant.

Lily
I don't really remember my dad. Apparently, that's a good thing. I remember Gramps though.

He was like an oak tree when I was a little girl, and he was so tall he went right up to the sky. When I sat on his knee, I was the safest girl in the world.

He taught me how to play guitar. If not for him, I'd probably have a career by now.

There's lots you can't do when you're in a band. It's like a calling. Not like living in a convent and giving up sex and nice clothes and all your independence. More like living in the back of a van and giving up your privacy and comfortable sleeping arrangements, and any hope of a steady relationship, and fresh food, and the idea of not being spotty when you're twenty-six.

Don't get me wrong, it's totally worth it for those crowds of forty or so people who just stare or nod their heads. I still love it.

Gramps tried to get me into flamenco, Hank Marvin, and Simon and Garfunkel. All I wanted to do was play Slipknot.

And then I heard Elvis for the first time. And I still just wanted to play Slipknot.

Then I grew up and left home, as you do.
He got old and went into a home, as you do.
I never thought that when I got older, he would too.

He's like a butterfly that's turning back into a caterpillar.
I just thought he'd be strong forever.
And since Mum died, we're the only family each other have left.
We're finding our way and he's doing his best.

I just want to pour all my feelings onto his lap,
but he wouldn't know what to do with them.
He can't do that
whole thing of saying how he feels,
so we chat about Easter or the weather,
but never anything real.

I hate coming here and seeing him get smaller each day,
but at least I can pour some of it out to you while I wait for him to get ready.
I don't even know your name,
or what kind of person you used to be,

but you never judge. You don't break my confidence or tell me what to do. And you never interrupt me to over-explain things. You're genuinely like no other man I've ever met.

Anyway, I better go to the lounge. I bet he's ready now. See you next time, strange, silent, listening man. Best therapist I ever had… only therapist I ever had. I can't afford a therapist, I'm in a band. See ya. *(Exits.)*

Enter Cyril.

Cyril
How did it go?

Neville
Oh… very well. She thinks you're great, all the usual. She's just gone to find you.

Cyril
What was that about the caterpillar and butterfly?

Neville
You've helped her spread her wings, erm, you know, musically. She's a rock star and she's very good at it. You're her oak.

Do you think she'll get the hump if she ever finds out that I'm not, you know… *(Waggles his finger at his head.)*

Cyril
Well, you are.

Neville
I don't know why you can't just talk to each other.

Cyril
She likes talking to you. You don't judge her like I do.

Neville
And what was with all the flamenco folky stuff? You should have gone down the Jimi Hendrix route, or, you know, Deep Purple.

Cyril
You don't really do culture, do you, Neville?

Scene Five

Cyril
Patrick, the orderly, is what they call a "stoner". He has three different states of being. One: stoned. Stoned and happy. This is the first hour or two of his shift.

Patrick
(Smiles for a while, then looks confused.) What?

Cyril
Two: grumpy. This is when he is not stoned. This is most of his shift.

Patrick
What do you want now? Oh, your insulin?

Cyril
Three: happy again. This is towards the end of his shift, when the prospect of getting stoned tends to perk him up.

Patrick
I might as well give you your sleeping tablets now. It'll be dark soon… ish.

Cyril
The good news is that we control Patrick.

Neville
That's right. Last month, we became suspicious when we noticed a sudden improvement in his mood halfway through his shift.

Cyril
And, low and behold, we caught him getting stoned by the bins.

Neville
We've been blackmailing him with the photograph.

Cyril
Unfortunately, we weren't able to take a photograph. Neville's fingers were shaking and I can't see very well.

Neville
However, Patrick doesn't know this.

Cyril
So far, he's procured us a bottle of Jim Beam, some homemade lasagne and a box of Ativan tablets.

Neville
You only told me about the Ativan.

Cyril
Patrick is our friend.

Scene Six

Patrick and Belinda are in their office. The buzzer sounds.

Belinda
Sandra's room. Get that, Gavin.

Patrick
So go on, Belinda. How did it go with the inspection?

Belinda
We got an outstanding! Excellent care, first-class facilities, highly dedicated staff. Gold stars all the way.

Patrick
Really?

Belinda
No! We're inadequate. We've got three months to get our act together or they're closing us down.

Patrick
Bastards.

Belinda
You're telling me! We did so much to prepare for that inspection. We cancelled the bingo, the trip to the garden centre, Sandra's ninetieth birthday *and* the safety training. What more do they want?

The buzzer sounds.

Both
Gavin!

Scene Seven

Neville is looking vacant.

Lily
My band's playing Monsters of Death on Saturday. The metal festival. *The* metal festival. Everyone's saying it's this really great opportunity, but I just feel terrified. Maybe I chose the wrong life because a music teacher once told me I was good.

You know what? If Gramps could hear what I actually did, he'd feel ashamed. He likes all the fancy plinky plinky plonky stuff and I play for a metal band called Abscess. God, he'd *hate* it. Maybe he's right.

Neville
He might not hate it.

Lily
(Jumps up.) What the fuck?!

Neville
Ooo! I'm having a rare moment of lucidity. It happens now and again. No, ah, no, it's gone. *(Snaps back to his previous state.)*

Lily
You've got to be shitting me! You were pretending? All this time?

Neville
Not all the time. The first time you spoke to me, I'd had a couple of Ativan tablets and I wasn't able to do a great deal. The dribbling was completely authentic. And then, over the course of what was, by anyone's standards, a fairly one-sided conversation, you just assumed that I was at a later stage than I actually am.

Lily
And then you go and tell everything to Gramps! You're his spy, basically.

Neville
That's not true. I only tell him what makes him happy.

Lily
Yeah, right.

Neville
Well, I do have a bit of a condition. It's not Alzheimer's, it's the other one, so in a year or two I might not remember what you've said anyway. If it helps, quite a lot of the time you were talking I did actually just zone out.

Lily
You're just like every other man I've ever met. You were definitely better when you were gaga.

Neville
Maybe most of us are. Anyway, you two should talk to each other.

Lily
Well, I'll definitely be talking to him today!

You can't tell him what I said about how much he'd hate my band: the him being ashamed of me thing. Please? You can't tell.

Neville
Of course.

Scene Eight

Neville
Anyway, she thinks you'd be ashamed of her.

Cyril
Oh. Well, she never mentioned that when she just tore a strip off me. Well, you've buggered it all up, haven't you? I'd like anything Lilly played; you know that.

Neville
I don't think you would, you know.

Cyril
I'd like the fact that she was playing it.

Neville
No, you wouldn't.

Cyril
She said she'll never visit me again.

Neville
Well, it serves you right.

Cyril
You said she was playing at a heavy metal festival?

Neville
Well, if that's what I said, then, yes, I definitely said that.

Cyril
And it's called Monsters of Death?

Neville
If that's what I said.

Cyril
Are you sure?

Neville
Sure of what?

Cyril
Well, let's assume you're right. Did she happen to mention what her band were called?

Neville
Ah. You've got me there.

Cyril
Come on, man. Think.

Neville
Sputum? Something like that?

Cyril
Sputum?

Neville
It was something gurgly.

Cyril
Patrick? You like terrible music. Have you heard of a heavy metal festival called Monsters of Death?

Patrick
Yeah, dude, it's huge. It's out near Lincoln.

Cyril
Another reason to hate Lincoln.

Neville
I know that part of the world. I used to be in a biker gang.

Cyril
Just run that by me again, Neville.

Neville
I was in a biker gang. In fact I was in charge, I ran it with my friend. I think his widow still lives round that way with their son, Trevor. He's a nice boy.

There's a lot you don't know about me, Cyril. In fact, these days there's a few things I don't know about myself. Hey… are you thinking what I'm thinking?

Cyril
I doubt it. I'm actually thinking.

Neville
I mean am I thinking what you're thinking?

Cyril
I dunno. I was thinking of asking Patrick to teach me how to work this phone, and then maybe I can find her music and listen to it. Then I could write her a letter and tell her how much I like it, even if I don't.

Neville
You won't.

Cyril
And then maybe I could watch her at the festival on the internet telly.

Neville
I was thinking we could go and see her in person: Lily! In Sputum! At Monsters of Death.

Cyril
Leaving aside the stupidity of this particular idea, which I'm very happy to come back to, they'd never let us go in a million years. By the time it's been risk assessed and pontificated on, A, we'll have died of old age, and B, they'll say no.

Neville
We could just go.

Cyril
For God's sake.

Neville
We can ask Patrick to give us his swipe card. And then, when they're not paying attention, which is all the time, we can just walk out, and we'll work everything out on the way and it'll be great.

Cyril
That'll be a step too far for Patrick. His mum's lasagne is one thing, but his swipe card? No. It's a terrible idea. Besides of which, it's not completely awful here.

Gavin (recorded voiceover)
Hello, pop pickers! Welcome to Primrose House FM. I'm

Gavin and here's everyone's favourite smoochy one: Jennifer Rush!

Jennifer Rush's 'The Power of Love' plays.

Cyril
Okay, let's go.

Scene Nine

Patrick
What? No, dude. No way. Come on, that's way too heavy for me, I could lose my job for that kind of shit. Look, I'll get my mum to do you a pecan pie.

Cyril
Come on, Patrick. It's more for Neville really. He loves his heavy metal. Did you know he used to run a biker gang?

Patrick
No, Cyril. Look, I like you both, but you blackmailing me is sort of shitty.

Cyril
Would you like to know the truth, Patrick?

Patrick
What do you mean?

Cyril
You remember when we caught you getting stoned by the bins and you saw us take that photograph? It was beyond our wits. We failed to take the photograph. Neville's fingers were shaking and I can't see very well. It was a bluff. We've got nothing on you.

Patrick
Wow… Hey, thanks for telling me, dude.

Cyril
Patrick, you are a good man and life is too short to be a prick to people. To be fair, it took me the best part of eighty years to work that one out, so we'll forgive you for being a little bit

behind in this respect. But I'm asking you, from one prick to another, please help us do this. Give two silly old fools the opportunity to have one last amazing experience; one last chance to actually *be* alive. Because one day, Patrick, this could be you.

Patrick
Shit. Aw, I'm sorry dude. I really want to… I do, but… I need to be a hard ass about this one. It's a no. Sorry.

Cyril
So, the Patrick-shaped tit of generosity has finally run dry, has it? Is there no human kindness left?

Patrick
I'm sorry, Cyril. You know how it is.

Cyril
I do. Anyway, after a bit of perseverance, it's quite easy to get the hang of all that camera-on-the-phone malarkey, isn't it? Do you know it does videos as well? Look, here's some footage of you giving Neville that box of Ativan tablets. Now, besides getting sacked, stealing tablets would be a criminal justice issue, unless I'm very much mistaken?

Patrick
(Produces his swipe card.) That's really fucking shitty.

Cyril
Sorry. You know how it is. *(Snatches Patrick's swipe card.)*

Oh, and it's a yes to the pecan pie.

Act Two

The Journey

"No man is ever old enough to know better."
Holbrook Jackson

Scene Ten

Cyril and Neville meet centre stage. Cyril presents the swipe card but won't let Neville touch it. They start running.

Both
Belinda!

Neville distracts Belinda by tapping her on the shoulder. She turns in the opposite direction. Both continue running.

Cyril uses the swipe card, and both enter the rotating door. Cyril does half a rotation, goes through the door and waits for Neville. Neville completes another rotation before being abruptly stopped by Cyril. They leave Primrose House.

Neville
Hey, Cyril, there's a bus stop!

Cyril
Nooo bus stop…

Scene Eleven

Patrick
It's crap being Patrick, 'cause that's me.
I always do my best to make people happy
and they have to go and make it hard.
And then they take your swipe card.

Belinda hit the roof.
She got me and Gavin to go through their rooms.

Cyril's was as clean as a pin.
He'd definitely been expecting us.
I worked this out from the note saying "Fuck off, Patrick"
he'd left in his underwear drawer.
Neville's room was poor.

'Cause of his crap memory,
he'd written everything down,
including the name of the festival,
how to get there,
what bands he's going to see
and what days they're playing,
but, 'cause of his crap memory,
he forgot to take it with him.

He left it on his bed and Gavin found it.
He gave it to Belinda. She totally lost her shit
about us being closed down and sacked;
and the long and short of it
is we're going to Monsters of Death to get them back.

Belinda got the tickets
and refunded herself from the petty cash,
and now we're on our way with a tank full of gas.

And although I am most undeniably stoked
that I might get to see Oozing Wound on their first UK tour,
I am pretty sure
that Belinda's going to knacker the vibe.
I've tried warning Cyril, 'cause I am still on his side,
but the daft old sod isn't answering his texts.
I'm a little bit worried about what might happen next.

Scene Twelve

Cyril
This whole thing was a terrible idea.
What the hell am I doing here?
And you're no use.

Neville
I'm sorry we're lost, but I think it's a bit mean of you to blame it all on me. I thought it was very kind of that Nottingham Forest fan to give us a lift. He might have taken us all the way there if you hadn't shouted "Blue Army". Anyway, I had an idea.

Cyril's phone pings.

Cyril
My phone went ding!

Neville
Your phone went ding.

Cyril
(Pulls his phone out.) It says, "Text message from Patrick." Do you do text messages, Neville?

Neville
I don't have a telephone.

Cyril
Well, I don't. They're a silly idea. He'll ring me if it's important.

Anyway, what am I supposed to do? Learn bloody Google? Find directions to Monsters of Death, purely just by virtue of…

Google (recorded voiceover)
Loading directions to Monsters of Death Festival.

Both stare at Cyril's phone and then at each other.

Google (recorded voiceover)
In six hundred yards turn right.

Cyril starts walking.

Neville
Ooo, I'll just, erm…

Cyril
Surely you don't need to go again?

Neville
I don't know when I'll next get the opportunity. I have to say, Cyril, I'm very impressed at how long you've been without going. It's extraordinary. *(Walks towards the corner.)*

Cyril
Thank you, Neville. On the downside, I might need to empty my catheter at some point. *(Aside.)* The malfunctionings of my waterworks are not something of which I'm proud.

So, what was your idea?

Neville
What idea? Oh yes!

(Turns around, having forgotten he needed the loo.) I had a good idea a few days ago, but then I forgot it. What a waste of a good thought.

Cyril
What?

Neville
Well, I remembered that I'd had this good idea, but I had no idea what it was; I'd just remembered that I'd forgotten. But while I was trying to remember it, I thought of a new good idea. It might be the same as the last one. We'll probably never know, unless I remember the old one, but then I might forget this one. It's a good idea.

Cyril
I think it's a terrible idea and you've not even told me it yet.

Neville
He's a nice boy, though. He may be able to help us. Please could I borrow your telephone?

> *Cyril hands Neville his phone. Neville looks at it and hands it back.*

Neville
Would you be kind enough to put me through to directory enquiries?

Scene Thirteen

Neville
Well, Trevor, look at you, all huge and handsome. You haven't half grown.

Trevor
I was twelve, Nev.

Neville
Still, well done. You're like a proper person and everything. Hold on a moment… Yep. You've got your dad's nose.

Trevor
You've hardly changed, except you're very old and nearly dead. I thought you'd still have your bike for some reason.

Neville
I did have my Triumph until a few years ago. Then they told me I couldn't be trusted, so I don't ride anymore. I don't drink either. I know.

Trevor
What's taking your mate so long?

Neville
Cyril's always had issues with urinating. It's a complicated process, particularly if there's a field of cows looking at him.

Trevor
Do you ever tell anyone about what you and my dad used to do?

Neville
No. Everyone back there sees me as this content, slightly befuddled old fella. Oh, I am. They're right.

Trevor
You don't tell them?

Neville
No. What's done is done.

Snaps to Neville and Cyril. Cyril looks distracted.

Neville
Oh yes, I used to run a biker gang.
We went round the country on motorbikes for about twelve years.
We saw AC/DC, Deep Purple, partied with Sabbath,
and did a lot of different drugs through a variety of orifices,
and had sex of varying quality
with several random people.
Sometimes we'd get into fights,
and we might have sold several things on the side.
We had some hairy moments,
but it was a wonderful time.
And then I settled down and became an estate agent.

Cyril
Sorry. Were you talking?

Snaps back to Neville and Trevor.

Neville
I think it's more dignified to keep your own counsel.

Trevor
I looked up to you loads when I was a kid.
I didn't know half of what you and Dad did.

Neville
And you've followed in his footsteps, by the look of things?

Trevor
Yep. So, the festival's over there,
about a ten-minute drive away.
There's a lock-up pretty close to the delivery gates.

A word to the wise:
these are serious guys,
but you are a bit of a legend from when my dad was alive;
so we've got you some leathers
and some T-shirts and bandanas.
I think they're about your size.

We had a conversation with festival security,
and certain people on a certain shift
won't look too closely in the back of a certain delivery lorry.

Neville
Thank you, Trevor. You've become an excellent middle-aged criminal.

Trevor
You've gone and lost that chip on your shoulder.
You were proper scary.
I thought you'd be a right piece of work when you got older.

Neville
You can thank the old brain condition for that one.
It's caused me to see things a little bit differently.

All that anger seems to have been knocked out,
along with a modest amount of my memory.
I tend to listen before I talk these days.
I'm slowly becoming a better version of me.
I'd recommend it as a lifestyle choice:
the occasional self-illuminating cerebral catastrophe.

Now I can generally find contentment,
whatever life churns up,
whereas take old Cyril:
sharp as a button! Miserable as fuck.

Trevor
One more thing: don't call me Trevor. It's Spider these days.

Neville convulses in mirth.

Trevor
Stop it.
Just keep your mouth shut and everything'll be fine.
My mum's made a packed lunch for both of you.
She says you need to need to come over and stay with us next time.

Scene Fourteen

Belinda and Patrick are in the car. Belinda is driving and Patrick is in the back seat. We'll assume Gavin is in the passenger seat.

Patrick
Are we nearly there yet, Gavin?

Belinda
So, these bands would break their instruments? On purpose?

Patrick
Oh, Belinda, it was great.

Belinda
That's awful. I dropped my recorder once at school and I had to stand in the corner and think about myself. Genesis wouldn't break their instruments, would they, Gavin?

Patrick
Well, they should do. Anyway, I'm going to get high right now, if that's okay with you two.

Belinda
What?

Patrick
Well, I've done this festival a couple of times and they do a pretty gnarly search on the gate, and so anything I don't smoke is going to have to go in the amnesty bin, and you'll see a grown man cry. So, to stop that from happening, I've rolled

everything into a very big carrot and I'm going to get high, if that's alright with you two. *(Lights and inhales.)*

Belinda
(Coughs and waves away smoke.) You could have just hidden it somewhere outside the festival!

Patrick
Oh, I didn't think of that, sorry. *(Inhales again.)*

So… how many gerbils do you think you'd need to take down a badger?

Scene Fifteen

Trevor
I remembered old Nev was an Iron Maiden fan,
so we got him a Number of the Beast T-shirt
and he was a very happy man.
His mate didn't seem very impressed.

Cyril
What the fuck is Napalm Death?

Trevor
I should have slapped him really,
but no one likes a bully,
so we just put the pair of them on the back of the flatbed lorry.

We get them to hotch right up to the back
and load up the gas canisters around them.
It takes about twenty minutes,
'cause they're heavy as shit.
Then we have to take them all off again,
'cause Nev needs a piss.

Neville
(Offstage.) Sorry!

Trevor
So we're late going through the gate,
but they wave us through without us having to wait.

We unload the canisters
and this pair of characters.
I shake Nev's hand and wish them both well.
You're at Monsters of Death now, fellas.
Welcome to the party.
Welcome to hell.

Act Three

The Festival

"Youth is the most precious thing...
what a pity it has to be wasted on the young."
George Bernard Shaw

Scene Sixteen

Cyril and Neville wander through the festival. Cyril points at Metalhead. Metalhead opens a bottle with their teeth, drinks from it, vomits, and then drinks again. Cyril and Neville continue wandering.

Neville points at Guitarist. Guitarist plays a solo. Cyril and Neville continue wandering.

They both point at Headbangers. Headbangers bang their heads and make the 'rock on' hand gesture. Cyril and Neville wander off.

Scene Seventeen

Volunteer
So, after coming here for a number of years,
I thought I might as well volunteer.
You get in for free, so you save a few quid,
and people are more deferential when you're wearing high vis.

I used to pick litter. Then I got trained in first aid,
so now I can just sit here and while the day away.

It's quite a pleasant evening
and things are generally uneventful,
so I decide I might as well buy myself an edible.

I pick my way past all the different tents,
the twenty-four hour café
where I sometimes go for coffee and brandy,
awash with those with more beer than sense;
and I find the annual spot where the Menu Man frequents.
I stand next to his tree and there he is,
like the shopkeeper from Mr Benn.

Enter Menu Man.

Volunteer
I'm sure he's got a pact with the devil.
He never seems to stop,
but he's increasingly forgetful
and he looks like a decomposing Iggy Pop.

Menu Man
Hello. You looking for anything?

Volunteer
Out comes his menu on a piece of string.

Menu Man
I've got Mexican mushrooms and LSD,
synthesised psilocybin pellets and peyote,
some weed called Crackdog and some MDMA,
and some slime scraped from the back of an Amazonian frog
that my mate Colin hand raised.
He had some last week and he forgot what words did,
so if that tickles your pickle, it's yours for twenty quid.

Volunteer
So I'm on my way back to the first aid tent
with my weed-flavoured jelly,
when two very old-looking men come up to me
and ask if I know of a band called Sputum.
Nope! Never heard of them.

I give them a shrug and off they trudge.
I wouldn't have thought of them again,
but then some other people come up
and say they're looking for their lost elderly relatives.
And yes, I might have seen them,
but I don't know where they went.

Scene Eighteen

Cyril
Scunthorpe on Halloween would be paradise after this place.
We've tried asking for Lily, but there are too many piercings.
When they said metal festival,
I didn't realise they meant all the stuff poking out of your face.

Why do people do that to themselves?
What do they call it? "Goth"?
We've just spent twenty minutes talking to one of those
and I still don't know whether it was a man or a woman…
or both… or neither…
I'm frankly at a loss.

Neville's gone to get a hotdog,
so I told him to wait for me there.
He knows this world much better than I do.
He went to great lengths to warn me about the portaloos,
but I was completely unprepared.
I wasn't going in there.

So I decided to cross over
to the comparatively charming four-way plastic urinal
operated by a foot pump,
and see if I could have a go
at emptying my bag into one of those.
Then along came these two biker blokes,
(Enter Biker Bloke, holds Cyril.)
who helped me hold my leg in the air.

They were surprisingly good company as it happens.
The conversation was quite lovely.
I managed not to mention the terrible state of their hair,
and, as far as I'm aware, neither of them mugged me.

Exit Biker Bloke, enter Patrick.

Cyril
So I'm walking back to the hotdog van,
feeling relatively chipper,
when I bump into bloody Patrick,
who's as stoned as a kipper.

It's inexplicable.

Patrick
Dude, it's totally… plickable.
We've come to take you back.
I've been trying to give you the heads-up.
You need to get out of here, and you know; good luck.

Cyril
Hold on. Who's "we"?

Patrick
Oh, Belinda and Gavin are here. They've just gone to get a hotdog.

Cyril
They've gone to get a hotdog?

Scene Nineteen

Neville
Someone shouts. I turn around
and there's Belinda
coming towards me through the crowd
with Gavin behind her.
That's a nice surprise, seeing those two here. *(Starts waving.)*

Cyril
I grab Neville's arm and pull him into the crowd.

Neville
Oh, we're avoiding them? I see what you mean now.

We head deeper into the field full of fans,
all highly motivated by this particular band.
It's getting quite dangerous under everyone's feet.

And in a sudden flash of clarity,
which is rare for me, to be fair,
I realise the quickest and safest way to get from here
to over there…

There isn't really time to explain to Cyril how crowd surfing works,
so I just ask him to trust me and do what I do.
I'm confident he will.
Then I get some obliging Ozzy fans to give us both a leg up.
And we're off!

Over the top of a leathery hairy hill
of flesh and arms and hands,
with the sunlight rolling around me.
I'm being carried closer to the band.

I wonder what Cyril's thinking? I turn around
and to my horror
I see the staff from Primrose House surfing towards us on the crowd…

Belinda
Arrgghh!

Neville
They're being carried along like rafts on a river.
I ask the people below me to please go quicker.

Then a pause in the music sends a flutter to my heart.
This can only mean one thing: mosh part.

The hairy sea suddenly erupts.
Belinda and the rafts all get sucked
into a human whirlpool,
while we're tossed around on a sea of luck.

I hope Cyril's had chance to empty his catheter.

Cyril exits.

Two burly men pull me over the stage barrier,
but of Cyril, there's no sign.
I hope he's alright, wherever he is.
He's a clever fella. I'm sure he'll be fine.

Scene Twenty

Cyril
I'm recovering in a tent
that sells overpriced coffee and stinks of incense.

The most important thing at the moment is the ownership of a settee.
There's nowhere to sit that isn't rock-hard or wet,
so I watch and I wait,
and as soon as someone vacates
their place, I'm straight in,
and now I'm not budging.

There's no sign of Lily, or whatever her band's called,
and now I've lost Neville and that can't be good.

And I'm not normally one to bother my Lord and Saviour,
but I send a small prayer heavenwards,
just to ask for one fucking favour.

Then this strange old man sits next to me without a bye or leave.
He gives me a smile and says I wouldn't believe
the day he's had.
Then he reaches into his bag
and shows me a menu on a piece of string.
Then he asks if I want anything
and produces a sheet of blotting paper.

Menu Man
A man of your age shouldn't pass into the next life
without experiencing the visual finery this thing has to offer.

Cyril
Now normally, I'd tell him to bugger off,
so that's what I do…
(Turns to Menu Man.) Bugger off.

But he doesn't flinch,
and so I have myself a think
and decide to hear him out.
And he opines…

Menu Man
A tiny square of this paper will open your mind
to possibilities you don't currently know about.

Cyril
Like how to find Lily in this terrible festival?

Menu Man
Yeah… Also, it'll be good for you, 'cause it's actually medicinal.

Cyril
Maybe it's because I'm desperate,
or I've been sensible for too long,
but I'll have a bit of paper.
What can possibly go wrong?

Scene Twenty-One

Belinda
Is this supposed to be a hot dog? It's pitiful.

Patrick
I've had three of them.

Belinda
Nice of you to join us, Patrick. Where the hell have you been?

Patrick
I couldn't find you.

Belinda
Well, while you were busy not finding us, we were the victims of a riot. I was scared for my life. Gavin had to go to the first aid tent. They were useless. Not nearly as useless as you, though. You're a waste of oxygen.

Patrick
Would this be a good time to ask for a reference?

Belinda
What did you say?

Patrick
Well, I thought I might apply for the activity coordinator job. I've had loads of great ideas. We could do art and crafts, film nights, wine tasting...

Belinda
Shut up. Activity? Don't make me laugh. You're about as active as a mummified sloth. You spend all day just chatting to residents as it is.

Patrick
You don't fancy my chances then?

Belinda
I tell you what, Patrick, you are *done* working for us. You're sacked, as of now, effective immediately. It's high time you started trying to make some friends your own age, rather than hanging out with the decrepit.

Patrick
Is that an Oozing Wound album?

Belinda
Don't get clever with me. You're the one who lost his swipe card and I'm the one clearing your mess up. That's why I am where I am and you're always going to be a loser who lives with his mum, even after she's dead.

Patrick
Fair enough. I might as well get more high then.

Belinda
Well, you can't, can you? You smoked it all in the car.

Patrick
Oh, ye of little faith. *(Reaches into his sock, pulls out a spliff, uncurls it, lights up and inhales.)*

Scene Twenty-Two

Neville
The band were so impressed with me crowd surfing at my age
that they asked the burly men to bring me backstage,
and I've been treated like royalty.
They have an excellent toilet. I've used it already.
Twice!

I've spent the last hour chatting with the singer.
His words are slurred, but he's a thoroughly nice man.
I get the impression he thinks I'm a fan.
I don't know him from a bar of soap.
Still, like I say, thoroughly nice bloke.

Rock Star
If you scattered people with your brain condition around this place,
you wouldn't be able to tell who had it and who didn't,
'cause, basically, everyone's off their face.

Neville
I can't grasp much of what he's saying,
but he thinks I can, as far as I can tell.
He looks at me and laughs a lot,
and I laugh back and it seems to be going well.

Rock Star
Of course, I'm always getting recognised,
so sometimes I like to put on a disguise
and just walk around the festival.

If I did that now, would you like to join me at all?
We might be able to find your mate.

Neville
Oh, yes please. That would be great.

Rock Star
I like seeing the little bands,
'cause they remind me of when I was starting out as a young man.

Neville
This makes me think of Lily,
and it starts a thought in my brain,
going backwards, like a train
reversing into a forgotten recess.
And then I remember Lily's band is called Abscess.

I must find Cyril and tell him without further ado.
Poor old Cyril.
I wonder what he's getting up to?

Scene Twenty-Three

Trippy visuals appear on the screen. Enter Cyril on his hands and knees. Eventually, he stands up and looks around.

Cyril
The man with a menu on a piece of string
gave me a thing that caused my soul to sing.
It was just a square of blotting paper,
but I swear upon my Saviour,
I never knew those patterns were there.
I was always unaware

of the textures in the tents and shirts,
the swirling shapes and outbursts
of colour in the crowd.
I look up at the clouds
and they are doing things I'll always remember.
Can no one else see this?
I should have brought my camera.

I had an excellent conversation with a fascinating goth.
I had no idea if they were a man or a woman…
or both… or neither.
And then I realised it doesn't matter a jot.

Enter Neville.

Cyril
Then I see Neville while I'm in some water,
and he's talking about things I don't quite understand.
He really is an excellent man.

Suddenly I start to laugh,
because, yes, he might be Neville,
but there's no one quite as daft
as us… me…

Neville
Him.

Cyril
Quack.

Scene Twenty-Four

Neville
We've just found Cyril talking to some ducks in the river,
like a demented Doctor Doolittle,
laughing at the clouds above
and telling us all about the colours he loves.

Cyril
Blue.

Neville
So we coax him to the bank and let him have an Ativan.
Then we sit and listen to him chatter on for a bit,
and half an hour later, it seems to have done the trick.
Sort of.

Cyril
Neville, you are a great waster of time. Note that is not the same thing as a great *waste* of time. In fact, quite the contrary, you are an excellent person to be spending one's time with! Maybe because you are so good at wasting it.

Neville
It's not quite the Cyril we know and love,
but I think he'll be okay.
Then I introduce him to my rock star friend
and tell him Lily's band is on tonight in the Snakebite Tent.

Cyril's response doesn't make much sense,
but I think he's got the gist.
All we have to do is get there in one piece,
and maybe convince him that these ducks aren't his.

Scene Twenty-Five

Lily
We're all set up and ready to go on.
The sound man's a nice guy,
but the stage manager's a moron.
He doesn't really give a toss.
We've got about a hundred and fifty
metalheads looking shifty,
and a few other people who look a bit lost.

We walk out to a smattering of applause.
I nervously say hello and play the first chords
of Black Lung.
I wrote it in high school and the first time I sung
it, I felt myself come alive.
Even now in this little tent, I can feel it in my spine.

So I burst into energy and scream across the stage.
I fly into a rage and sing about the dead.
Some people in the crowd are banging their heads…

There's an old man at the front who looks a bit like Gramps,
except he's got a Napalm Death T-shirt and a sloppy grin on
his face.
Gramps wouldn't be seen dead in this kind of place.

Hold on, that's his friend next to him.
The one from the home who pretended his brain had gone.
And he's just started a mosh pit. What the hell's going on?

Scene Twenty-Six

Lily
Have you slept?

Cyril
Oh yes.
Neville took me to the trailer of his rock star friend
and gave me another Ativan.
I slept like a log and now I feel a new man.
Anyway… I liked your band.

Lily
You what?

Cyril
I thought you were very accomplished.

Lily
What was your favourite song?

Cyril
Well, erm, I particularly enjoyed "Genital Meatgrinder." That was in the key of C, wasn't it? And the chap on the bass doing the backing vocals; his voice was extraordinary. It sounded like he was vomiting gravel.

Lily
Wait a minute. Just stop. This is too weird.
Do the people at the home even know you're here?

Cyril
Oh yes.
I think they'll be talking to us.
But today we'll see some bands that Neville likes.
I owe him that much.
I'm sure they'll be shite.

This rock star,
whose name Neville has so comprehensively failed to grasp,
has given us both an accessibility pass:
access to the podium by the mixing desk,
with an excellent view of everything.
Neville says his friend can't even sing.

Lily
Who is this rock star? Do you know?

Cyril
I'm afraid I couldn't tell you,
but he thoroughly enjoyed your show.

Lily
I thought you'd hate us. I thought you'd feel ashamed.

Cyril
I loved it.

Lily
Really?

Cyril
Yes. Partially because I was on drugs. In fact, as I was pondering the clouds this morning, which will never look the same again after last night, I realised that for the first time ever, I feel content. Not as fuckwittedly so as Neville, but I've got

no unfinished business. You're alright, Lily. I'm very proud of you. Do you think you'll come and visit us soon?

Lily
Only if we're going to talk properly and Neville stops pretending he's past it.

Cyril
One day he won't be pretending.
And I might run out of things to say.

Lily
I might just visit you anyway.
I really thought you had no surprises left.
I can't believe you're into Napalm Death.

Scene Twenty-Seven

Neville
Well, what an experience. It's been simply wonderful.
I wonder if I can talk Cyril into coming to next year's festival?

Cyril
No! Okay, maybe.

Neville
The rock star treated us to an excellent meal, and we're walking towards the viewing platform with our accessibility passes.

I turn around and, in the distance, I see
the care home staff with festival security.
They start running towards us and it's only fair to say
Belinda's at risk of spoiling my emotional feng shui.
Me and Cyril swap glances and decide to run away.

Cyril
When I was young,
I could outrun
just about anything with legs
and several things with wheels.
Now here I am, aged eighty-two,
being chased through
an overcrowded field full of people in leather.
Even the bald ones need a haircut…

… and as they pass the security man and head up the ramp,
we start climbing up towards the speaker stack.
Neville gives me a smile and says there's no going back.

I take a moment to look around.
I've never seen so many people,
pulsating as one to the most terrible sound…

Neville
It's such a blue sky.
I'll settle for that if this is it.
Down there is the mosh pit:
a human tsunami of balmy testosterone…

We look down at the crowd and then at each other.
Can we make it?

Cyril
Let's give it a go.

And as our pursuers come towards us,
we throw ourselves into the air
and fly down towards all that filthy denim.

Neville
I can't see Cyril, but I'm glad I'm with him.

Epilogue

"Nothing fucks you harder than time."
Davos, Game of Thrones

Neville is looking vacant. Cyril is next to him looking grumpy. 'Invisible Touch' by Genesis is playing.

Patrick (recorded voiceover)
And that was Genesis: Invisible Touch. That song goes out to Cyril and Neville, who are back from hospital after doing something a bit silly the other week. It's also dedicated to Gavin and Belinda, who left our team recently. As we know, this was Belinda's favourite song, and we wish them both every success with finding employment.

Invisible Touch ends with a scratch. Neville and Cyril start smiling.

Patrick (recorded voiceover)
Anyway, so that's the last time we'll ever hear that.

So, after the wine tasting on Sunday afternoon, Cyril and his granddaughter will be playing flamenco for us. Film night tomorrow is… well, some of you wanted Brief Encounter and some of you wanted Halloween, so we thought we'd thought we'd play half of each.

Don't forget, next week, we'll be welcoming a new resident! We don't have his actual name yet, but he's known as the

Menu Man, and apparently he's prepared some recipes for us, so that should be exciting.

This next track goes out to today's visitors: Spider and his friends from the biking fraternity, who befriended some of us on a recent field trip. Thank you for all the cider and please come again.

> *AC/DC's 'Highway to Hell' starts playing. Neville and Cyril turn and look at each other, tap their feet and make the 'rock on' hand gesture.*
>
> *Newspaper clipping appears on screen with the headline 'Multi-Platinum Selling Rock Star Says She Owes It All to Granddad'.*

The End

Production Notes

AWOL is written to be performed by two or three people with a projector screen.

Actor #1: Cyril
Hastings
Belinda
Lily
Trevor
Menu Man
Guitarist
Rock Star

Actor #2: Neville
Patrick
Metalhead
Volunteer
Biker Bloke

Option of a third person playing Belinda, Lily, Volunteer and the Menu Man/Ma'am.

Optional interval at the end of Scene 14, with Belinda announcing that there's a services coming up and she could do with a break.

Feel free to adapt the region-based jokes to your own locality.

AWOL uses several music tracks, but only those integral to the dialogue feature in the script.

Please ensure your venue has professional licensing for any recorded music used.

Acknowledgements

I owe an enormous thanks to my friend **Jon Paterson** for helping to nurture this show since its inception, as well as inhabiting the characters on stage in such a glorious and nuanced way. I'm also grateful for his skills as a tech and lighting designer. Oh, and the posters. In short, whether we're in Adelaide, Orlando or Vancouver, I couldn't ask for a better touring partner.

Ryan Gladstone took the reins as director and brought the show to life. Besides his natural flair for the comedic and sublime acting notes ("Patrick is still angry, but with added crushed hope"), I'm particularly grateful for the edits he suggested for the script – they raised the bar no end!

Steve Escott and I have done rural touring together in the UK for many years. He does all the hard work – driving, lighting and sound – while, for my part, I go on stage and fanny around for a bit. I want to thank Steve for the hours he's spent listening to me gibber on in his passenger seat, as well as for his tech input, easygoing nature and badly hidden joie de vivre.

I'm also grateful to him for suggesting **Stuart Tavendale** to perform this show with me in the UK. An actor of immeasurable talent and tremendous fun to work with, Stuart is extremely flexible and a consummate pro. Going on stage with him is like riding a bike with stabilisers.

I'd also like to thank **Mantle Lane Press** for being a joy to work with, and **Matthew Pegg** for his unerring patience and excellent eye for book design.

Last but definitely not least (I wouldn't dare), love and thanks to **Gemma**, my partner, best friend and unofficial carer, who makes even the crappest day delightful and somehow finds it within herself to listen to all the repeated drafts.

And thanks for reading this far! Stay great and remember: in a world of Cyrils, be more Neville.

Rob